The Origins of Nunn-Lugar
and Cooperative Threat Reduction

The Origins of Nunn-Lugar and Cooperative Threat Reduction

by Paul I. Bernstein and Jason D. Wood

Center for the Study of Weapons of Mass Destruction
Case Study 3

Case Study Editors: Jeffrey A. Larsen and Erin R. Mahan

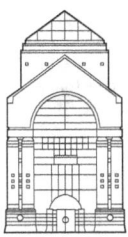

National Defense University Press
Washington, D.C.
April 2010

NDU Press publications are sold by the U.S. Government Printing Office. For ordering information, call (202) 512–1800 or write to the Superintendent of Documents, U.S. Government Printing Office, Washington, D.C. 20402. For the U.S. Government On-Line Bookstore go to: www.access.gpo.gov/su_docs/sale.html.

For current publications of the Institute for National Strategic Studies, consult the National Defense University Web site at: www.ndu.edu.

Contents

—

Prologue: From Silos to Sunflowers

The collapse of communism in Eastern Europe and the USSR in the two short years from 1989 to 1991 shook the underpinnings of international security structures and challenged the policy priorities of nearly all of the world's governments. No preparations for a transition were (or perhaps could have been) made in advance. The Soviet empire shattered into fifteen unequal fragments.

—Sam Nunn and Richard Lugar, 1995[1]

In a 1999 interview, Ashton Carter, a key figure in helping to create and implement the threat reduction program initiated by Senators Sam Nunn (D–GA) and Richard Lugar (R–IN), recalled four visits between 1994 and 1996 to an intercontinental ballistic missile (ICBM) base in Pervomaysk, Ukraine. Planted in the soil of this base were the most powerful rockets mankind has ever made, armed with hundreds of hydrogen bombs and aimed at the United States. In turn, Pervomaysk was itself the target of similar American missiles and weapons. Under the Nunn-Lugar program, the missiles deployed at Pervomaysk by the Soviet Strategic Rocket Forces and the silos that housed them were destroyed. As Carter recounted:

[W]*hen we first went there we helped with removing the warheads from the missiles. That was the first step. Then we went back again, and we removed the missile from the silo . . . and destroyed the missile. The third time we went back, we blew up the silo and restored the site. And the fourth time, and the time I'll never forget, is when Secretary of Defense Bill Perry, Russian Minister of Defense Pavel Grachev, and Ukrainian Minister of Defense Valery Shmarov planted sunflowers atop that place where a missile silo carriage holding a missile carrying ten warheads, brand new ones, designed for us, had once been. Instead, they planted sunflowers.*[2]

How had it become possible to transform a missile field into a sunflower field within the lifetime of those who had grown up during the height of the Cold War, when the United States and the Soviet Union aimed at each other tens of thousands of nuclear warheads deployed on submarines, ICBMs, strategic bombers, tactical aircraft, and numerous battlefield delivery systems? The unmatched destructive power of these weapons required that rigorous safety and security measures control their design parameters, production methods, transport, storage, and use. But as the Soviet Union dissolved in 1991, deteriorating political and socioeconomic conditions gave rise to concerns over the future security of the Soviet nuclear arsenal. What measures were in place to prevent the misuse or diversion of Soviet nuclear weapons, their design information, and related materials or technology?

Anticipating the possibility of loosely controlled nuclear weapons inside the former Soviet Union, key leaders in Congress and experts in the policy and academic communities began to assess the nature of this threat and to consider approaches to reducing the danger it posed to U.S. and global security. Out of these investigations emerged the initial Nunn-Lugar legislation and the broader Cooperative Threat Reduction program—an unprecedented effort to reduce nuclear dangers by securing or eliminating Russian weapons systems and related materials and capabilities using aid from the U.S. Government.

How did Nunn-Lugar come to be? Who were the key leaders, facilitators, and practitioners who recognized the need and opportunity—at a pivotal moment in history—to pioneer a program of cooperative security between two former adversaries? What key insights and lessons can be drawn from the origins of Nunn-Lugar? To answer these questions, this case study recounts initial attempts to aid the former Soviet Union, describes the events leading to the passage of the Nunn-Lugar legislation, and reviews early efforts by the Senators to facilitate implementation of the program.

Sam Nunn: Longstanding Concerns about Nuclear Security and Risk Reduction

The creation and passage of the Nunn-Lugar legislation occurred quickly over a period of weeks after the Cold War ended, but the concerns about managing nuclear risks that animated Sam Nunn extended back two decades. His discovery in the early 1970s of serious deficiencies in the security of U.S. tactical nuclear weapons based in Europe was a formative experience that left him "thoroughly shaken" and committed to critically examining the safeguards that had—and had not—been in place to reduce the risks attending the deployment by both sides of many thousands of nuclear weapons and the way in which the superpowers practiced nuclear deterrence.[3]

Later that decade, Nunn's concerns about the risks of nuclear war beginning accidentally led him to question U.S. nuclear planners about their ability—and that of Soviet planners as well—to determine with high confidence the origin of a ballistic missile strike directed at either country. Disturbed by what he learned from the Strategic Air Command (SAC), Nunn partnered with Senator John Warner (R–VA) to champion the establishment of Nuclear Risk

Reduction Centers in Washington and Moscow that would facilitate communications and help minimize misunderstandings that could create or exacerbate a nuclear crisis.[4] Nunn's concerns about this issue persisted into the 1990s, leading the Department of Defense to undertake a major review of the accidental launch problem that resulted in a number of largely classified risk reduction measures.[5]

A Pivotal Meeting with Gorbachev

These experiences were prologue to the chain of events that began in August 1991, which would greatly heighten Nunn's sense of urgency about nuclear security and broaden his vision regarding the scope of action required to address the emerging problem. That month, a small group of hard-line government and military leaders in Moscow placed Soviet President Mikhail Gorbachev under house arrest in an attempted coup. While the coup failed, it further destabilized the Soviet polity and accelerated its dissolution later that year. The political crisis engulfing the Soviet Union led some in the West to worry about the security of its vast nuclear arsenal, which was stored in four of the Soviet republics and deployed on Soviet submarines at sea.[6]

That same month, while attending an Aspen Institute conference in Budapest on developments in the Soviet Union, Nunn was invited to visit Moscow to meet with Gorbachev and other officials.[7] According to Nunn, "Just after President Gorbachev was released from house arrest following the failed coup, [I] met with him in his Kremlin office, and asked him directly if he had retained command and control of the Soviet nuclear forces during the coup attempt."[8] Specifically:

> [O]ne of the key things on my mind was the status of the nuclear briefcase, the nuclear control device in the personal possession of the head of the country. Had Gorbachev really been in command throughout the coup attempt? Did he maintain total control over the Soviet Union's nuclear weapons? I had met with Gorbachev on a number of previous occasions, and his answers to these questions did not have the same ring of conviction as his statements during our earlier meetings. It seemed to me that either he was not himself clear about the status of command and control of nuclear weapons during that crucial period, or he was not comfortable discussing the matter candidly with me.[9]

Either way, "[t]he Soviet Empire was coming apart. I was optimistic that this breakup would expand freedom and reduce the risk of global war, but I left Moscow in the early fall of 1991 convinced that it would also present a whole new set of dangers."[10]

Nunn-Aspin: The First Attempt to Aid the Soviet Union

These dangers demanded action if the risks of instability and "loose nukes" were to be managed effectively. But there was also opportunity embedded in these dangers. As Nunn and Lugar later put it, U.S. policy grew "out of the realization that history had offered an unusual opportunity: the ability to enhance U.S. security with the cooperation and goodwill of the most lethal former adversary of the United States and at the same time enhance the security of the world's newest democracy and assist it with badly needed political, economic, and military reforms."[11] After his visit to Moscow, Nunn was convinced that Washington had to do all it could to help the Soviet leadership maintain control over its nuclear weapons. Nunn soon called for funds to be authorized to assist the Soviet Union in converting its defense establishment. He also called for confidence-building measures and military exchanges as part of an effort to put in place quickly some measures that could shore up stability in the Soviet military and convey Washington's goodwill and support of a safe transition to a post-Soviet world. At about the same time, Les Aspin, Chairman of the House Armed Services Committee (HASC), had developed a separate proposal to provide humanitarian aid to the Soviet Union.

Aspin's package was in addition to nearly $3 billion in food and agriculture assistance that the George H.W. Bush administration had provided to Gorbachev's government earlier in 1991. He proposed redirecting $1 billion in fiscal year (FY) 1992 defense funds to provide food, medicine, and other types of humanitarian assistance to Moscow. Aspin tied this assistance directly to nuclear security: "During the Cold War, the threat was deliberate Soviet attack. Now, the bigger threat seems to be chaos in a nation with 30,000 nuclear weapons."[12] To Aspin, investing what amounted to less than one-half of one percent of the defense budget to the cause of stabilizing what most agreed was a highly dangerous situation was a sensible—indeed, compelling—way to advance the Nation's security.

Not everyone agreed. In recounting reaction to Aspin's proposal, Nunn and Lugar later noted that Secretary of Defense Richard B. Cheney referred to it as "foolish," and that President Bush stated, "I'm not going to cut into the muscle of defense of this country in a kind of an instant sense of budgetary gratification so that we can go over and help somebody when the needs aren't clear and when we have requirements that transcend historic concerns about the Soviet Union."[13] Influential legislators in both parties echoed this view, arguing against spending money to assist the Soviet Union. Nunn and Lugar note that many House members feared that Aspin's initiative would establish a dangerous precedent for reprogramming defense funds for nondefense purposes that would remain under HASC control—an idea that was not popular with other House committees.[14]

Nunn, however, shared Aspin's sense of urgency and saw an opportunity to join forces to advance both their initiatives in Congress. As both the House and Senate Armed Services Committees had proceeded to conference to reconcile their respective FY92 defense authorization bills, Nunn and Aspin agreed to combine their proposals into a single new initiative. This amendment would authorize the expenditure of defense funds to provide Moscow with humanitarian aid; technical assistance to safely transport, store, and dismantle nuclear and chemical weapons; and assistance in defense conversion, environmental cleanup of defense sites, and training and housing for decommissioned officers of the Strategic Rocket Forces.[15]

Nunn, Aspin, and those supporting their amendment referred to it as an "anti-chaos" initiative or an "insurance policy" that constituted "defense by other means." Senator Carl Levin (D–MI) argued that it presented "a chance to bury the new Hitlers and Stalins of that region before they have a chance to take root."[16] Despite adamant opposition from House and Senate Republicans, particularly over its provisions related to training and housing decommissioned Soviet officers, the Nunn-Aspin amendment was approved by the two defense authorization panels and added to the FY92 defense authorization bill—but only after straight party-line votes in both committees.[17] The White House was not enthusiastic about the amendment but chose to not openly oppose it as long as it did not *mandate* assistance to the Soviet Union—that is, as long as the authority to expend the funds was discretionary.[18]

In November 1991, the authorization bill faced a tough vote on the House and Senate floors. At this point, domestic politics intruded. As recounted by one of Nunn's key staff aides, "[j]ust before the defense authorization bill reached the Senate floor, Harrison Wofford, a Democrat, won a formerly Republican seat in a special Pennsylvania election, largely on the basis of an 'America first platform.' Wofford's successful dark horse candidacy sent an anti–foreign aid shock wave through the House and Senate. This development, added to Republican opposition to specific aspects of the package and the absence of active White House support, caused the Democratic leadership in both the House and Senate to remove the Nunn-Aspin legislation from the FY 1992 defense authorization bill."[19]

Reflecting on the unusual effort to introduce the amendment so late in the legislative process, Nunn later observed, "We did not get away with it."[20] Aspin and Nunn had not conferred with even Democratic lawmakers until the last minute, let alone the Republican minority. Moreover, they did not have the support of the White House, which played no role in crafting the legislation. Procedurally, some claimed the measure circumvented the normal foreign assistance authorization process, which Aspin acknowledged as contributing to the effort's demise. Rather than face defeat of the entire conference report, Nunn and Aspin withdrew the amendment.

Still, they had succeeded in raising awareness of the nuclear security issue, and important advocates emerged for the need to consider a more systematic and robust approach to the matter of assistance to the Soviet Union.[21] But a new approach to developing a legislative consensus was needed.

Toward Nunn-Lugar

A new approach began to take shape almost immediately after the demise of Nunn-Aspin. Two critical factors helped sustain the momentum. The first was the decision by Richard Lugar to join forces with Sam Nunn to champion nuclear security assistance to Russia. Like Nunn, Lugar was deeply engaged in international security and nonproliferation issues and concerned about developments in the Soviet Union. Widely respected in the foreign policy arena, Lugar was a senior Republican on the Senate Foreign Relations Committee and therefore in a position to provide bipartisan leadership on the question of giving financial assistance to Moscow.

The second factor was the assessment of the Soviet nuclear arsenal recently completed by a team of Harvard analysts. This study, *Soviet Nuclear Fission: Control of the Nuclear Arsenal in a Disintegrating Soviet Union*, was a systematic examination of exactly the problem that Nunn, Aspin, and now Lugar had been worrying about.[22] On November 19, 1991, just 6 days after withdrawal of the Nunn-Aspin amendment, Ashton Carter, the study director, briefed the findings to a small group that included Nunn, Lugar, a few of their staff aides, William Perry of Stanford University, John Steinbruner of the Brookings Institution, and David Hamburg, president of the Carnegie Corporation, which had funded the Harvard study. In Carter's words, "The study predicted that the breakup of the Soviet Union posed the biggest proliferation threat of the Atomic Age and outlined a new form of 'arms control' to stop it: joint action by the two former Cold War opponents against the common danger."[23] One of Nunn's key aides later wrote of the Harvard team, "Their conclusion was carefully reasoned and profoundly disturbing: political and economic instability in the Soviet Union could have grave consequences for the safety and security of Moscow's nuclear arsenal, particularly if the Soviet Union divided into autonomous republics."[24]

Soviet Nuclear Fission lent empirical and analytic weight to the argument Nunn had been making for several months and validated the urgency he attached to the need to adapt policy to confront the security dangers that political turmoil in the Soviet Union posed. The report provided substantial background information on the entire Soviet nuclear weapons enterprise, to include the nuclear command and control system—what the authors describe as "the anatomy of the problem." As the authors noted, "dangers of illicit diversion of key weapon-related technology do not end with the non-strategic and strategic deployments alone but extend to fissionable materials, components, delivery systems, and command and control systems."[25] The point was clear: the nuclear security and proliferation risks emanating from the disintegrating Soviet state were multidimensional and complex. "Loose nukes" had become the shorthand for this challenge, but far more than the weapons themselves was at issue.

The study examined specific threats that could result from deficiencies in Soviet nuclear safeguards and controls and suggested a range of measures to improve these controls and thus ensure safe custody of Soviet (and post-Soviet) nuclear weapons during a period of political transition. These measures ranged from inventory and data exchange to weapons dismantlement, disposal of special nuclear materials, and even contingency plans for the recapture of stolen weapons.[26] The authors believed that U.S. assistance could be instrumental in implementing many of their recommendations.

Additionally, the Harvard study documented the lack of nuclear capacity in the Soviet republics that were to become newly independent states and inheritors of Soviet nuclear weapons. The authors noted that "of the republics of the Soviet Union, only Russia has within its borders anything like the technical means necessary for full-cycle operations and maintenance of a nuclear arsenal to world standards."[27] The United States, they argued, had a significant stake in ensuring that the political settlement attending the dissolution of the Soviet Union not result in several new nuclear weapons states in the region. Not only would such states lack the knowledge or capability to exercise responsible control, but their possession of nuclear weapons could well be a destabilizing factor in the Eurasian region.

The impact of the November 19 meeting was instantaneous. Nunn and Lugar were reinforced in their commitment to revive the key elements of the Nunn-Aspin amendment, and the work to draft the new legislation began that day.[28] Nunn and Lugar convened a followup breakfast meeting 2 days later that included a bipartisan group of 16 senators. Carter repeated his briefing of the Harvard study. Recalling the opposition that had doomed Nunn-Aspin, the two Senators later remarked, "Once acquainted with Carter's analysis, these colleagues agreed that U.S. domestic political hostility to Soviet aid paled in comparison to the dangers in question."[29] In the discussion that took place that morning, Nunn and Lugar gathered the support of the senators in attendance for a $500 million proposal to provide assistance for the safe transport, storage, destruction, and nonproliferation of Soviet weapons of mass destruction (WMD).[30]

Nunn and Lugar next turned to the task of building public support for their initiative. Their November 21 op-ed piece in the *Washington Post*, "Dismantling the Soviet Arsenal: We've Got to Get Involved," outlined in terse, urgent language the WMD danger posed by the Soviet breakup and the imperative to respond with a program of assistance that was not so much a handout to a longtime adversary as an act of enlightened self-interest and an investment in America's own national security. They noted: "Cooperation with Soviet authorities on destroying nuclear and chemical weapons should not be postponed. The benefits of responding are too great, the dangers of inaction too severe. We believe Congress must act now to authorize a program of cooperation with the Soviet Union and its republics on the destruction of these weapons."[31]

The Nunn-Lugar legislation was offered as an amendment to an unrelated bill. Titled the "Soviet Nuclear Threat Reduction Act of 1991," the amendment had 24 cosponsors and was adopted in the Senate by a vote of 86–8 on November 25. To Nunn and Lugar, this vote represented the most dramatic reversal of opinion they had ever experienced in the Senate.[32] On November 27, the House of Representatives adopted the measure by acclamation. President Bush signed it into law on December 12, 1991, 4 days after the first formal steps were taken to dissolve the Soviet Union.[33]

The law states: "The program . . . shall be limited to cooperation among the United States, the Soviet Union, its republics, and any successor entities to (1) to destroy nuclear weapons, chemical weapons, and other weapons, (2) transport, store, disable, and safeguard weapons in connection with their destruction, and (3) establish verifiable safeguards against the proliferation of such weapons."[34] The legislation did not appropriate new funds to the Department of Defense. Rather, the Pentagon was given the authority to transfer (or reprogram) $400 million from existing accounts, and it did so from Operations and Maintenance accounts.[35]

A number of conditions applied to implementation of the legislation. The most challenging of these with respect to gaining passage were "performance criteria" pushed by Senator Jesse Helms (R–NC), Chairman of the Senate Foreign Relations Committee. Helms sought language that would require the President to certify that recipients of Nunn-Lugar aid were complying with six conditions, to include compliance with all relevant arms control agreements and observance of internationally recognized human rights, including the protection of minorities.[36] Certifying such compliance would have been difficult, if not impossible, for the post-Soviet states that were just forming. Discussions at the staff level yielded a compromise that required recipients to be "committed to" comply with the six conditions. This compromise cleared the way for passage of the legislation.[37]

Following Through in 1992

Having achieved the unlikely feat, over the course of just a few months, of directing several hundred million dollars to help a nation that for decades had been the mortal enemy of the

United States, Senators Nunn and Lugar and those who had helped them understood that their work had just begun. To be sure, it was now the job of the executive branch to craft specific policies and programs to implement the intent of the legislation. And the Bush administration had begun to mobilize to initiate implementation of Nunn-Lugar: a number of high-level visits to the region had yielded a range of proposals for specific programmatic activity; a senior level coordinator and negotiator had been named; and allies had been approached about a coordinated effort to assist the Soviet successor states. Still, by March 1992, the Senators were concerned that there had been insufficient progress in developing a concrete plan to use the Nunn-Lugar funds, despite calls from the leaders of Russia and other former Soviet republics to begin the process of destroying WMD and converting defense enterprises.[38] Moreover, they believed, as did a number of their Senate colleagues, that it was important to monitor carefully the post-Soviet political situation and the progress of the Newly Independent States (NIS).

In March 1992, Nunn and Lugar led the first of two Congressional delegations (CODEL) to the NIS that were important in helping to establish assistance priorities, accelerate the provision of aid, and expand the scope of the Nunn-Lugar program. The report of the March CODEL urged that Nunn-Lugar funds be used for a number of specific purposes that would enable progress in WMD dismantlement. It was important, the report noted, to avoid focusing exclusively on nuclear dismantlement in Russia; as urgent as this task was, it was also critical to work with other NIS governments and not lose focus on the requirements of chemical weapons dismantlement. The report also recommended a number of steps to accelerate the process of defense conversion. Equally if not more important, the report highlighted what for Nunn and Lugar was a principal conclusion of their visit: the need for a comprehensive U.S. strategy for helping the NIS that encompassed not just WMD dismantlement, but also economic development, especially steps to remove Cold War restrictions on commerce and encourage private sector investment.[39]

The recommendations in the CODEL report became one of the foundations of the assistance plan developed by Secretary of State James Baker and his team. Nunn and Lugar recount briefing President Bush on their trip:

> *The president opened the meeting by noting that he was lukewarm about the idea of trying to get a major assistance package for Russia through the Congress in an election year. After a thorough vetting of the report's findings and recommendations and Secretary Baker's comments on the State Department's review of basic components of an assistance package, however, the President decided that this*

opportunity to assist the reform process in the states of the former Soviet Union should not be missed. He asked the secretary to put together a comprehensive legislative aid proposal for consideration by the Congress. The president also said he would give strong personal support to the proposal.[40]

That proposal became the Freedom Support Act, signed into law in October 1992. This legislation added $400 million in Nunn-Lugar funding and expanded Nunn-Lugar authorities in the areas of defense conversion, military-to-military contacts, environmental cleanup, and housing assistance for displaced nuclear officers. An additional $105.8 million provided for humanitarian and development assistance to be managed by the U.S. Agency for International Development.[41]

In November 1992, shortly after the election of William Clinton, Nunn and Lugar led a second CODEL. In the intervening months, the economic situation in Russia had deteriorated significantly, posing a danger to the economic and political reforms being pursued by Russian President Boris Yeltsin and raising questions about whether the United States and other Western powers were sufficiently committed to the reform process and prepared to deliver all the financial aid that had been promised. Against this backdrop, the CODEL met with seven heads of state in seven countries.[42] As Nunn and Lugar later recounted:

The connection between economic stability and international security became very clear to the CODEL. Hyperinflation and conservative backlashes could overwhelm the advance toward market economies and political democracy. Economic deterioration could lead to dissolution of control over nuclear weapons. Control over conventional weapons had already disintegrated in some areas. All of these threats would become more pressing if U.S. attention and assistance waned.[43]

The November CODEL report reiterated the March report's call for more active government involvement to encourage private sector investment in the NIS. This was an urgent priority for national security reasons but also one that would pay economic dividends later.

The CODEL was equally concerned by what it found with respect to nuclear security. As Nunn and Lugar later observed:

The multiplication of weapons-related threats in the newly independent states was striking. . . . the threat of a single unauthorized launch or nuclear weapon accident had clearly grown. Senior Russian military officials told the delegation of their concern about the safety of, and central control over, strategic nuclear weapons deployed in Ukraine. They warned that the situation was "deteriorating" and that it could force Russia to renounce responsibility for the safety of those weapons.[44]

The fact was that one nuclear state had been replaced by four—each, in the Senators' words, with "severe internal economic, political, and ethnic strains." Fortunately, the "nuclear inheritor" nations—Belarus, Kazakhstan, and Ukraine—reaffirmed to the CODEL their strong desire to remove nuclear weapons from their territory. However, they lacked the means, expertise, and resources to accomplish this. The CODEL report emphasized the importance of the prompt, safe dismantlement of strategic nuclear weapons, the ratification of the Strategic Arms Reduction Treaty by all parties (after which the dismantlement process could be accelerated), and the accession of Belarus, Kazakhstan, and Ukraine to the Nuclear Nonproliferation Treaty as non–nuclear weapons states.

The danger that worsening economic conditions and persistent WMD security problems could feed on one another and produce a catastrophic outcome led Nunn and Lugar to conclude that the United States needed to focus greater attention to developing and executing the integrated national strategy for the NIS they had first called for after their March visit to the region. This blueprint for relations with the post-Soviet nations should be organized, they argued, under a single senior level coordinator reporting directly to the President and secretary of state.[45]

The election of Clinton to the Presidency in 1992 set a course for Nunn-Lugar that likely would have been quite different had George H.W. Bush been reelected. As the Clinton administration came to power early in 1993, the appointments of Les Aspin as Secretary of Defense, William Perry as Deputy Secretary, and Ashton Carter as Assistant Secretary with responsibility for the Nunn-Lugar program signaled the strong commitment of the new President to the objectives of Nunn-Lugar and allowed the cooperative threat reduction enterprise to become institutionalized in the Department of Defense. Carter established a new organization within his nuclear security and counterproliferation office dedicated to assisting the former Soviet Union and coordinating Nunn-Lugar activities.[46] And as the need for a more systematic, longer term effort became increasingly clear, cooperative threat reduction was granted its own line in the Defense budget for FY94. With a dedicated budget, funds no longer needed to be reprogrammed from other activities, and resource planning could become more predictable. The program was on solid footing.

Epilogue: Lugar Looks Back and Ahead

Speaking to his colleagues in the U.S. Senate on December 18, 2009, Richard Lugar reflected on the origins of the legislation that bears his name, the accomplishments of nearly two decades of cooperative threat reduction, and the challenges of the future.[47] He noted that as of December 2009, the Nunn-Lugar program had dismantled or eliminated 7,514 nuclear warheads, 768 ICBMs, 498 ICBM sites, 155 bombers, 651 submarine-launched ballistic missiles, 32 nuclear submarines, and 960 metric tons of chemical weapons.[48] All told, he observed:

> *The United States and Russia have eliminated more nuclear weapons than the combined arsenals of the United Kingdom, France, and China. In addition, American and Russian experts have worked together to remove nuclear material from vulnerable locations around the world and to secure it in Russia. In 2008, the last of the nuclear warhead storage facilities identified under the Bratislava Agreement received safety and security upgrades. In May 2009, the chemical weapons destruction facility at Shchuchye began its important work of destroying 2 million chemical munitions.*

He noted that beyond the sheer destruction of so much Cold War weaponry, "the cooperative links established by such activity and the confidence-building value inherent in our on-site presence are assets of incalculable value." He then pointed to the future, and to the logical progression of the process begun in 1991:

> *Beyond Russia, it is vital that we break new ground in safeguarding and destroying weapons of mass destruction. I have never considered the Nunn-Lugar Act to be merely a program, or a funding source, or a set of agreements. Rather, it is an engine of nonproliferation cooperation and expertise that can be applied around the world. And it is a concept through which we, as leaders, are responsible for the welfare of our children and grandchildren, as we attempt to take control of the global threat. . . . But the Nunn-Lugar program has demonstrated that the threat of weapons of mass destruction can lead to extraordinary outcomes based on mutual interest.* [49]

At the end of the Cold War, the Nunn-Lugar program provided the means to defuse a potentially serious threat, begin the process of reorienting U.S.-Russian relations toward greater cooperation, and enable the peaceful transition of the former Soviet republics.

Notes

[1] Sam Nunn and Richard G. Lugar, "The Nunn-Lugar Initiative: Cooperative Demilitarization in the Former Soviet Union," in Allen E. Goodman (ed.), *The Diplomatic Record 1992–1993* (Boulder, CO: Westview Press, 1995), 140.

[2] Public Broadcasting System, transcript of "Russian Roulette: Inside Russia's Nuclear Complex, Comments on the Nunn-Lugar Program," 2, available at <www.pbs.org/wgbh/pages/frontline/shows/russia/arsenal/lugar.html>.

[3] The NATO episode is recounted in remarks given by Nunn at the Monterey Institute for International Studies on August 20, 1995. These remarks, "Changing Threats in the Post–Cold War World," were included as the foreword in *Dismantling the Cold War: U.S. and NIS Perspectives on the Nunn-Lugar Cooperative Threat Reduction Program*, ed. John M. Shields and William C. Potter (Cambridge, MA: The MIT Press, 1997).

[4] Ashton B. Carter and William J. Perry, *Preventive Defense: A New Security Strategy for America* (Washington, DC: The Brookings Institution, 1999), 70–71.

[5] This review was conducted by the Commission on Fail Safe and Risk Reduction of the Nuclear Command and Control System (also known as the FARR Commission), established on April 24, 1991, and chaired by Ambassador Jeanne Kirkpatrick.

[6] John Felton, *The Nunn-Lugar Vision: 1992–2002* (Washington, DC: The Nuclear Threat Initiative, 2002), 5.

[7] Nunn and Lugar, "The Nunn-Lugar Initiative," 141.

[8] Sam Nunn, "Moving Away from Doomsday and Other Dangers: The Need to Think Anew," speech at the National Press Club, Washington, DC, March 29, 2001.

[9] Nunn, "Changing Threats in the Post–Cold War World."

[10] Nunn, "Moving Away from Doomsday."

[11] Nunn and Lugar, "The Nunn-Lugar Initiative," 140.

[12] Ibid., 142.

[13] Ibid.

[14] Ibid., 143.

[15] Richard Coombs, "U.S. Domestic Politics and the Nunn-Lugar Program," in Shields and Potter, 42.

[16] Jason D. Ellis, *Defense by Other Means: The Politics of U.S.-NIS Threat Reduction and Nuclear Security Cooperation* (Westport, CT: Praeger, 2001), 78.

[17] Coombs, 43.

[18] Ibid.

[19] Ibid.

[20] Nunn, "Changing Threats in the Post–Cold War World."

[21] These included former U.S. Ambassador to Moscow Jack Matlock, as well as Robert Strauss, who was Ambassador during the period of the dissolution of the Soviet Union and was the first American Ambassador to the Russian Federation, through November 1992.

[22] Kurt M. Campbell, Ashton B. Carter, Steven E. Miller, and Charles A. Zraket, *Soviet Nuclear Fission: Control of the Nuclear Arsenal in a Disintegrating Soviet Union* (Cambridge: Harvard University,

November 1991).

[23] Carter and Perry, 71. Perry would become Deputy Secretary and later Secretary of Defense in the Clinton administration. Carter would serve as Assistant Secretary of Defense for International Security Policy.

[24] Coombs, 43. Just a few weeks later, the Soviet Union was formally dissolved.

[25] Campbell et al., iii.

[26] Ibid., 42–47.

[27] Ibid.

[28] According to Carter, he and three key staffers (Robert Bell, Kenneth Myers, Jr., and Richard Coombs) "stayed behind to draft what became known as the Nunn-Lugar legislation." Carter and Perry, 72.

[29] Nunn and Lugar, "The Nunn-Lugar Initiative," 144.

[30] Nunn and Lugar note that during this period Viktor Mikhaylov, Soviet deputy minister of atomic energy, was meeting with members of the Senate to discuss Soviet problems with storing, destroying, and controlling nuclear weapons. Sergey Rogov and Andrey Kokoshin of Moscow's USA–Canada Institute also briefed Senators on nuclear control issues. See Nunn and Lugar, "The Nunn-Lugar Initiative," 144. These briefings presumably served to reinforce what some Senators had heard in the Carter presentation.

[31] Sam Nunn and Richard G. Lugar, "Dismantling the Soviet Arsenal: We've Got to Get Involved," *The Washington Post,* November 22, 1991, A25.

[32] Nunn and Lugar, "The Nunn-Lugar Initiative," 145. The Nunn-Lugar Amendment became Title II of Public Law 102–228.

[33] On December 8, 1991, the presidents of Russia, Ukraine, and Belarus signed the Belavezha Accords, declaring the Soviet Union dissolved and establishing the Commonwealth of Independent States (CIS). The Russian parliament ratified the accords on December 12, formally voiding the 1922 Treaty on the Creation of the Soviet Union. On December 21, the leaders of the other Soviet republics (with the exception of Georgia) signed the Alma-Ata Protocol, affirming the dissolution and acceding to the CIS. On December 25, Mikhail Gorbachev resigned as President and declared the office "extinct." On December 26, the Council of Republics of the Supreme Soviet recognized the dissolution. By December 31, institutions of the Soviet state had ceased operating.

[34] PL 102–228, Section 212, "Authority for Program to Facilitate Soviet Weapons Destruction."

[35] This "transfer authority" is found in Section 221 of PL 102–228: "The President may . . . transfer to the appropriate defense accounts from amounts appropriated to the Department of Defense . . . not to exceed $400,000,000 for use in reducing the Soviet military threat." Department of Defense leadership was not pleased at having to redirect defense funds "out of hide," especially for a program whose value they believed was questionable.

[36] See Section 211(b) of PL 102–228 for the six conditions.

[37] According to one participant involved in subsequent efforts to certify the commitment of recipient nations to the legislative conditions, it was another compromise, this one offered by the office of the Department of Defense General Counsel, that allowed implementation of Nunn-Lugar to move forward. Under this compromise, initial judgments of commitment to comply would be based on statements made by the new governments, while future judgments would be based on their actions. E-mail

exchange with Susan J. Koch.

[38] Nunn and Lugar, "The Nunn-Lugar Initiative," 146.

[39] Ibid., 147–148.

[40] Ibid., 149.

[41] The Freedom Support Act was formally known as the Freedom for Russian and Emerging Eurasian Democracies and Open Markets Support Act.

[42] Estonia, Latvia, Russia, Kazakhstan, Kyrgyzstan, Ukraine, and Belarus. See Nunn and Lugar, "The Nunn-Lugar Initiative," 150.

[43] Ibid., 151.

[44] Ibid., 150.

[45] Nunn and Lugar summarized their findings and recommendations in an op-ed in the *Washington Post*, "Still a Soviet Threat," December 22, 1992, A21.

[46] Carter named Gloria Duffy as Deputy Assistant Secretary of Defense and Special Coordinator for Cooperative Threat Reduction.

[47] Congress, Senate, Senator Lugar of Indiana speaking for the Fiscal Year 2010 Department of Defense Appropriations Act, H.R. 3326, 111th Cong., 1st sess., *Congressional Record* 155, no. 194 (December 18, 2009): S13410–13411.

[48] See "The Nunn-Lugar Scorecard—Destroying Weapons and Materials of Mass Destruction Through Cooperation," available at <http://lugar.senate.gov/nunnlugar/scorecard.html>.

[49] Ibid.

About the Authors

Paul I. Bernstein is a Vice President and Senior Program Manager with Science Applications International Corporation (SAIC) in McLean, Virginia. He specializes in analysis and project management in the areas of weapons proliferation, strategic forces policy, and regional security, and works with U.S. Government agencies on a range of research, planning, and professional military education activities. Mr. Bernstein is a member of the Combating WMD Panel of the Threat Reduction Advisory Committee, has supported development of key combating WMD strategy and concept documents, and has been a guest instructor at all senior Service war colleges and other professional military education venues. Recent publications include *Countering Weapons of Mass Destruction: Looking Back, Looking Ahead,* Center for the Study of Weapons of Mass Destruction Occasional Paper 7 (Washington, DC: National Defense University Press, 2009); "Combating WMD Collaboratively," *Joint Force Quarterly* 51 (4th Quarter 2008); and *International Partnerships to Combat Weapons of Mass Destruction*, Center for the Study of Weapons of Mass Destruction Occasional Paper 6 (Washington, DC: National Defense University Press, 2008). Mr. Bernstein holds a Master's Degree in International Affairs from Columbia University.

Jason D. Wood is a Policy Analyst with SAIC. His research in support of various U.S. Government agencies focuses on nuclear deterrence, arms control, security assurances, fourth-generation nuclear weapons, and deterring WMD terror attack. In 2010, Mr. Wood was selected to participate in the Nuclear Scholars Initiative, sponsored by the Center for Strategic and International Studies, where he is preparing a forthcoming publication on integrating nuclear, space, and cyber policy. Previously, Mr. Wood was a Research Associate at the Institute for Foreign Policy Analysis, researching national security space issues and missile defense. He has also worked as an independent consultant to Jane's Information Group, specializing in military command and control systems. Mr. Wood holds a Master of Science degree from the Missouri State University Graduate Department of Defense and Strategic Studies.

Center for the Study of Weapons of Mass Destruction
Case Study Series

Case Study 1
President Nixon's Decision to Renounce the U.S. Offensive Biological Weapons Program
by Jonathan B. Tucker and Erin R. Mahan
October 2009

Case Study 2
U.S. Withdrawal from the Antiballistic Missile Treaty
by Lynn F. Rusten
January 2010

For additional information, including requests for publications and instructor's notes, please
contact the Center directly at WMDWebmaster@ndu.edu or (202) 685-4234
or visit the Center Web site at www.ndu.edu/wmdcenter/index.cfm